I0122193

Your Story
Tales of Love, Tragedy, Despair, and Healing

Your Story
Tales of Love, Tragedy, Despair, and Healing

Howard Upton

Copyright © 2019 Still Water Literary, LLC

All rights reserved. No part of this publication may be reproduced or utilized in any form by any means, electronic or mechanical, including photocopying, recording, or by any information storage and retrieval system, without prior written permission from the publisher.

Library of Congress Cataloging-in-Publication Data

Upton, Howard, 1969-
Your Story, 1st Edition

ISBN – 978-1-946811-05-9

1. True story 2. Humanity 3. Faith 4. Psychology

Still Water Literary, LLC ™

Other works by Howard Upton

Action/Adventure

Of Blood and Stone: A Bill Evers Novel

Occam's Razor: A Bill Evers Novel

Humor

My Dog's P.O.V. and How He Sees the World

Author Contributions

Go Ask Your Dad by Dominick Domasky

Secrets of the Martial Arts Masters by Dr. Bohdi Sanders

To you, the man or woman, boy or girl, facing what others have not.

And to you, the man or woman, boy or girl, facing what others have, but in your own personal way.

This is your story.

Introduction

As far as career choices were concerned, I had always chosen wisely, or at the very least luck was with me as decisions were made. I once took a promotion, reluctantly-because it was two states away from home, only to learn three weeks later the facility I had left burned to the ground. Another time, I was promoted with a new company, once again leaving behind close friends and family. Only a few short months later a series of layoffs and plant closures ripped through my previous employer, and many of my former colleagues and friends were without work.

Believe it or not, climbing the corporate ladder had never been one of my career objectives. Opportunities presented themselves, and it seemed I was always in the right place at the right time. Life was good and my wife and I enjoyed excellent paying jobs. We owned and almost had our retirement home paid off in just under three years when I received another recruiting call.

"Howard, this role is perfect for you. The position is that of Vice President and the pay is in line with its title. Not to mention, the job is in Georgia (I was living in Pennsylvania at the time, and longed to get closer to my home state of Alabama). You'll oversee three plants and their quality systems programs," explained the job recruiter.

"What about the company? Is it solvent? What are its long range plans and strategic goals?" I asked. You see, the company was private and I had no access to its financial status as I would a publicly traded company.

"They're in a great position," he replied immediately. "The owner just purchased a third location in South

Georgia, and the other two facilities are performing very well. Future expansion is on the horizon. Everyone I've placed with this company has been very, very happy."

With those words of encouragement, I boarded a flight from Allentown, Pennsylvania and flew to Augusta, Georgia where I met with the owner of the company and one of the human resources managers. We sat for two hours discussing the opportunity, the business, and future outlooks. I was sold! These guys had it together and I would be able to move closer to home.

My wife and I discussed the opportunity and decided to take the plunge. We bought a second home in Georgia and were ecstatic with the endless possibilities. My first novel was due to be published right after our move there and her job was going well; we had the world at our fingertips!

At first things were wonderful, but then I began keeping up with the company's financials. Things were not nearly as rosy as I had been lead to believe; financially, the company was almost insolvent. I watched our accountants stress out every day and listened to our company owner scream about every silly mistake made that might cost the company a penny. Things were even more dire than I could have imagined.

I was afraid to tell Cathy about the financial position of the company, and believed deep down that our company's leadership team would weather the tumultuous times and eventually better position the business so it would prosper. By March, I could tell things were getting worse. Rumors abounded about potential layoffs. In April, a catastrophic event took the primary processing plant down for two days. I worked feverishly to provide documentation to the federal government to allow us to begin running again. Finally, the scientific data I supplied them was enough, but at that point, the two day loss of production time created a significant financial pitfall the company was incapable of overcoming. In early May, raw material pricing spiked.

By mid-May I began dropping hints to Cathy that I would probably be facing a layoff.

"They aren't going to get rid of you," she replied, "look at how much you've done for the company."

"None of that matters," I said. "All they will be looking at is how to cut overhead, and my salary is significant overhead. We need to prepare ourselves for this."

At the end of May, Human Resources asked that I meet with the company attorney who, in turn, notified me that the company was letting me go for financial reasons. I felt my heart sink. Cathy and I had two mortgages, were busy paying off some outstanding debt, but quite a bit of the debt remained. How could I face my wife who had put so much faith in my decision making?

To say that I felt like a failure would be to minimalize the emotions I was dealing with at the time. The half-hour drive home didn't give me much time to prepare for the conversation I was going to have with Cathy. Traffic was marginal, but I recall how irritated I was at everyone and everything. The world felt as though it was crumbling around and on top of me.

"What are we going to do?" Cathy asked.

"I don't know, but we'll be okay," I tried to reassure her.

I walked to the refrigerator and tried to find solace at the bottom of a beer. When that didn't work, I cracked another, then another. Only my dog Rex was oblivious to what was happening and wanted nothing more than a little affection.

I logged onto my home computer and began scrolling through the various social media sites hoping (honestly) to find someone else willing to share their problems so I might feel better about my own. The typical drivel pasted my monitor. Political ramblings, pictures of food, people happy the weekend had arrived, and the usual requests for unspoken prayers peppered my Facebook page. My cynical nature wanted to respond to every one of them with some snarky, juvenile comment, but I refrained.

Just as I was about to log off, a story posted by a friend of mine caught my eye. Rick discussed the painful decision he made to re-enter the emergency medical field after being laid off by his previous employer. His choice did not come without doubt and fear; having spent so many years in the field previously had forever etched within his mind the faces of the dead—men, women, and yes, children. He admitted to suffering from post-traumatic stress disorder as a result of his work, but because of his situation, he was forced to rejoin his old profession. "I have to put food on the table and take care of my family."

This declaration hit me pretty hard. The past several years of my career, and the resulting benefits, ran through my mind like an out of control locomotive. Yes, we had two mortgages, but we had the resources available to pay off our Alabama home. My vehicle was paid off, and Cathy's not far behind. Our children were taken care of and the possibility of moving home and renting out our Georgia home was the most plausible direction for us.

Was our situation as bad as I thought? My career progression and regression aside, I did not suffer from PTSD, and I was not at a point where I worried about how we would purchase the basic necessities of life. We were not homeless, and because of my background and relatively young age, I knew I would land a job soon enough, even it was not in the same financial stratosphere that my previous role provided.

Suddenly, I felt very selfish and dropped my head in shame--partially because what I was feeling was real, and partly because the beer was intensifying the emotion. I walked back into our living room and hugged Cathy then told her everything was going to be okay. She is an incredibly strong and intelligent woman and our conversation was productive. We discussed renting our Georgia home, paying off our Alabama house (that we affectionately referred to as "Green Acres"), and me finding work immediately. We both felt a sense of relief wash over us and moved forward with preparation for the move.

In the coming days, I thought more and more about Rick's situation and wondered how impactful his story would be to others dealing with their own struggles. I reached out and asked what his thoughts were about being featured in a project I was considering. Over the past year, I had been fortunate to have my first novel published and the second one scheduled for publication in the fall of 2015. Knowing about my recent success in the world of fiction, he agreed and answered a bevy of question I threw his way regarding his situation.

My questions were invasive, but he answered each one willingly and without compunction. I saw the beginnings of a new book—a venture into the inspiration genre and non-fiction: both outside the realm of my writing comfort zone. As with any good challenge, I elected to face this one head on.

The project was going to need more than this introduction and Rick's story, however, so I began reaching out to others who were facing or had faced crises and asked if they were willing to tell their stories, as intimate and delicate as they might be. Only one person turned down the opportunity, and she was a political refugee who was being pursued by her own government at the time. I could hardly argue with her desire to continue flying under the radar!

Within these pages are the stories of those who have been challenged, continue to be tested, fight to smile another day, survive to see the sun shine again, or simply leave their home without fear. These are *your* journeys; these are stories of everyday people heroes. Who needs Hollywood or Broadway when we are the ones screaming to be heard and understood?

Before you get the idea that these stories are heartfelt and altogether touching, let me assure you that some of them were extremely difficult for me to type. My wife often tells me that there are no tears in my body because she never sees me cry, but some of these stories, these tales of humanity on a grand scale, affected me in a way that is difficult to describe. I could sometimes feel the lump forming in my throat as I read from my notes and attempted to bring their tales to life. Other times I would wipe a wayward tear from my cheek, the pain their narratives conveyed affecting me in some way that felt abnormal and alien.

The stories are woven from discussions and personal writings sent to me by those who lived them. In some cases, I tell the tale from the third person; an omniscient writer who stares down upon an actor moving and talking as though in a play. Other times, I allow the story's owner to take the wheel and drive. In several cases, I choose to intersperse third person narrative with direct first person quotations. You are obviously an intelligent reader, and I've no doubt you will discern one from the other, but I felt as though particular liberties should be taken to convey each story to make them palatable and meaningful.

I tell you this not to insult you, but to prepare you for different perspectives whose life changing events were shared in their own way. Weaving tales together in first and third person narrative is generally frowned upon, but I felt it fit, and had I to do it all over again, I would not change a thing. These stories are given to you as they came to and for me.

Read on, savoring each tale while considering where you are in your own life. You may be better off than you first suspected!

Don't go looking for the reasons
Don't go asking Jesus why
We're not meant to know the answers
They belong to the by and by

~Chris Stapleton

Rick
Alabama

Rick was a young seventeen year old boy about to embark on the fast track to adulthood. While living in Birmingham he received a call from his mother telling him to come home—his father was terminally ill and was on the verge of passing away. He and his sister hopped in a car late at night and raced down Highway 280 toward Alexander City, a considerable drive from the small urban city of Birmingham.

Around one o'clock in the morning Rick and his sister Dianne happened upon a terrible car accident. His sister worked as an emergency medic, and as their car rolled to a stop, he watched as his sister morphed into the professional he had never seen.

Rick recalled the calmness that crept over her face as she examined the young man in the crashed car who was suffering from severe head trauma from slamming into the car's windshield. Dianne grabbed her personal trauma bag, crawled through the wrecked car and applied cervical traction while opening the man's airway. Her demeanor seemed detached from her normal self, the medical professional taking over her personality like a spirit taking over a living person's body and mind.

An ambulance, the police, and firefighters arrived at the scene and began cutting the young man from the destroyed car. He and Dianne returned to their vehicle and finished the drive to Alexander City, but that night would forever remain with Rick.

After finishing high school in 1981 and watching his father die from cancer, he began thinking about what he would do with his life. Faced with the normal dilemma that many young men face, Rick had to decide whether he would go to college or take up a trade of some sort. After looking into classes at a local community college, one in particular caught his eye: basic emergency medical technician.

Thinking back to the night when he and his sister encountered a tragic accident, Rick remembered Dianne and her calm resolve as she worked to save the man's life until the ambulance arrived. He signed up for emergency medical technician classes away, graduating one short year later.

Finding work was easy, and soon Rick was living his dream of being an EMT in Birmingham. For two years he worked three to five days at a time, sleeping at the station between calls. The pay was meager, but Rick was happy with his new profession. The men and women he worked with became his extended family.

After several years of working long, arduous hours something happened that would change Rick's outlook on life and his career—he and his wife had a son. Suddenly, the hours spent in ambulances and at the station became longer and harder. He missed his family and wanted to be home with them. His wife was a registered nurse, made considerably more money than he did, and worked eight hour shifts seven days a week. After working a full week, his wife was off work for seven consecutive days. As a result, Rick did what any rational person would do, he went to nursing school and became a registered nurse.

For five years, Rick worked as a registered nurse, but he quickly realized how much he missed being a medic. The adrenaline, the camaraderie, being in the middle of the action were the things that drove him to the medical field—that and the memory of his sister. Despite how much he missed working in the EMT field, Rick knew that going back was not an option. The money he made as an

RN was three times what he made as a medic, and supporting a family on twenty-five thousand dollars a year would not cut it.

Furthering his education, Rick went back to school and completed his bachelor's degree then promptly entered into a master's of nursing program. After graduation, he acquired employment with an exceptionally busy emergency department in Montgomery, Alabama as a nurse practitioner. The role was satisfying and paid very well. He spent much of his time ordering x-rays, suturing cuts and wounds, diagnosing illnesses and prescribing medicine.

It was here, however, that things began wearing on soul, mind, and heart. Rick relayed to me some of what he dealt with in the emergency room and trauma wards. Understandably, an individual coping with and witnessing death on a personal level was closely associated with a soldier on the battlefield.

"Over the years I performed cardio pulmonary resuscitation, or CPR, on numerous babies. Some of those babies were suffering from SIDS *(sudden infant death syndrome)*, some had been beaten by abusive parents, and others had been involved in tragic accidents. Many of those babies I watched die.

"I worked on teenagers who, when life had gotten tough for them, put a pistol in their mouths and pulled the trigger. Some of the teens hung themselves in their bedrooms. I recall once working a scene where a young teenage couple decided to die together from carbon monoxide poisoning. We found them holding each other in the front seat of a pickup truck—dead because their parents wanted them to break up.

"Children burned so severely that the only areas of their bodies left unaffected were the soles of their feet were rushed to the emergency room. I cared for other burn victims that received their injuries in house fires or car explosions."

Rick paused before continuing, "There was a two year little boy whose mother had hit him in the head with a heavy iron object because he wouldn't stop crying after she scalded him in a bathtub three days earlier. I watched her lie at the foot of the baby's bed crying and screaming…begging us to not stop trying to revive him.

"I remember every case, every face. Vivid details remain with me of calls where babies, young children, and teenagers died too soon, and the memories of their mothers and fathers staring me directly in the eyes begging God and me to keep their child alive. Cold, dark death came anyway, and each of their memories haunts my dreams, forcing me awake many nights sweating and chilled, my heart racing as a sense of panic overtook me.

"In 1995 I vowed to leave the emergency room and never come back. I was going to retire from medicine and work at Home Depot selling flooring where I could be happy. As luck would have it, my brother-in-law told me I should look into the Occupational Health Clinic at a major car manufacturer in Alabama.

"I was out of work, fifty-two years old, had two children, three foster children, and wanted to adopt. All of this on a meager salary was enough to apply for the position my brother-in-law told me about. I landed the job and was happy, but unfortunately, I was laid off."

Rick was at the proverbial crossroads in his life. He was forced to make a decision to re-enter the emergency room environment, bear witness to the trauma and tragedy he swore he would never allow himself to see again. As a result of his work situation, he defaulted to what he knew and applied for a job that paid well so he could provide for his own family.

I asked Rick about his mental state and was shocked at what he relayed.

"Yeah, I suffer from post-traumatic stress disorder. I can't temper my dreams. When they come and wake me, I get up and watch television or work out. The medication I take to help me with the depression also helps me manage my panic attacks. The thought of the state taking my kids away from me because I can't provide for them drives me. They are the reason I do what I do. If it weren't for them, I wouldn't care if I lived in a used mobile home and worked a low paying job, but because of them, I walked back into a job that haunts my sleep and scratches at the back of my mind when I'm awake."

Rick told me that he is a Christian man and believes God will bring him through any situation in which he finds himself. However, his inspiration and internal drive comes from his family.

He has embraced his role as husband and father, choosing to provide for his family in any conceivable way. While many men would turn away and refuse the challenge Rick has faced, he elected to walk toward the problem. Internal drive and tenacity are the building blocks of a sound and stable life; Rick has undoubtedly laid the foundation and built upon it!

This sort of commitment to one's family is not only inspiring, but also enviable. When you look in the mirror, ask yourself if you have what it takes to live among your demons and battle them every day to provide for your family. If the answer is yes, you are a mental warrior and should be commended!

Loranda
Nebraska

By all accounts, and according to Loranda, she was lost without her husband. LeRoy was quite literally her other half. Together they owned and raised cattle on their four hundred eighty acre ranch in the Sandhills of Nebraska. Far from civilization the couple shared everything together, LeRoy the pragmatic decision maker, Loranda the artist. In her words, "We lived life like we danced—we were awesome."

The two met at a bar in a small town. According to Loranda, LeRoy asked her out several times before she agreed to a date. LeRoy, by all accounts was a gentleman and a great dancer, but she was not looking for a relationship. At long last, however, she went out with him.

They would run into one another at his uncle's bar where LeRoy continued to pursue Loranda, but she continued to stay distant, her heart not into it. Eventually, she went out with him again, meeting and "hanging out" as she put it at a local town event. He told her while they were there that he had to leave for a little while to help his sister-in-law with some things, but he would return in a short while. Loranda waited and waited for him, but he didn't return. She thought that perhaps he had run into issues with his family, so she drove home.

The next day, while in town, Loranda overheard someone talking about "Shorty," LeRoy's nickname. He had been in an automobile accident on his way to his brother's house, rolling his pickup truck over and pinning his leg between the steering wheel and the top of the cab.

"It was then I knew I loved him," Loranda said.

The couple was married for eighteen years and seven months, those years passing quickly as they do for anyone recalling the loss of a loved one. LeRoy encouraged her to write, draw, paint, and play guitar. He loved her artistic side and purchased a used Les Paul guitar at a music store that she fell in love with after plucking a few chords.

"This can be my Christmas present," she told LeRoy. "What do you want for Christmas?"

"This *is* my Christmas present," he smiled, "because I get to hear you play."

Loranda confided, "LeRoy lived life full out, no holds barred, while I lived safely. He wasn't perfect, but the good so outweighed the bad that it wasn't work to be married to him."

The two lived and worked on their ranch before LeRoy was diagnosed with a serious illness. Thirty hours after the doctor told them of his sickness, he was gone. I asked Loranda how his death impacted her.

"Oh man, that is a tough one. For a long time I felt lost and did not know who I was without him. I knew who I was before LeRoy, but that person wasn't me anymore, and the person I became with LeRoy's love died with him."

Four years after LeRoy's passing, she began to find herself again. First, she began playing music again and also focused on another passion—her artwork. "We were together 24/7 working side-by-side. All the little things, all the jokes between us…," she paused.

"I'm still scared (of being alone), worried that I will do something wrong. I've always been willing to do the work so long as someone else was there making the decisions, but now it's just me. I think, in hindsight LeRoy spent our whole marriage preparing me to be without him. He forced me to do things that were out of my comfort zone. My only hope is that I made him as happy as he made me."

I asked Loranda what motivates her to push forward without LeRoy by her side.

"I have to…or need to, or maybe I just don't know what else to do. When I drove myself the two-and-a-half hours home from the hospital after LeRoy passed, I couldn't believe he was gone and how alone I was. It didn't seem real—how could it be real?

"When I got home, my mom and a friend were getting the house ready for company. I changed clothes and went out, got on the tractor and put hay out for the cows. There was comfort in the routine and caring for the animals that depended on us, regardless of what was going on in our lives. I knew that was what LeRoy would want me to do, so I pulled my big girl panties up and carried on."

It took Loranda time before she was able to pick up her guitar and begin playing again. She struggled with the idea of strumming those strings without her biggest fan there to hear her, but eventually she began to pick a few chords. Before long, she found herself playing in a band. Now Loranda focuses on her artwork, plays her music, and tends to the ranch that she and LeRoy spent so many years cultivating.

What separates an individual motivated to live on, even after the sudden and untimely death of their soul mate from those who have not experienced this type of loss? For eons, philosophers, psychologists, and laymen have wondered at the internal fortitude of some to push forward and live, even though a piece of them died with their loved one.

From an article appearing in Psychology Today entitled "Grief, Loneliness, and Losing a Spouse," Dr.

Romeo Vitelli explains, "...spousal bereavement is a major source of life stress that often leaves people vulnerable to later problems, including depression, chronic stress, and reduced life expectancy."

As many know, losing a loved one can be the most difficult situation to overcome mentally and physically. The toll that a person's death takes on those left behind can be debilitating, especially for those who have difficulty coping with the loss. For many, however, remembering a warm smile or quirky behavior helps to pull them from the mental abyss.

Perseverance comes from somewhere deep inside. What motivates us to move through and beyond a terrible situation is different for each individual. Some people look inward, while others seek God for help and peace, while others smile at a memory and strum their guitar.

Charlett Arizona

No one ever wants to feel the pain of losing a loved one, most especially that of a child. To contemplate such a loss sends shudders down our spines and gives way to a sickening feeling deep within your gut. Many of us know men and women who have lost a child, but most do not engage them in conversation about the death for fear of uncontrolled emotions both from the parent and from ourselves.

Charlett was awakened to an agonizing call at 2:00 AM, and her life has never been the same. She shares her story so each of us can understand and empathize with a mother who lost her son at a young age. Charlett also recalls her story so we can all reflect on the human spirit and its ability to overcome extreme loss and pain.

Charlett was a week shy of her twenty-first birthday when she gave birth to her son, Tyler. Her son was a good natured boy who loved to laugh. She described her son as funny and goofy, whose favorite day was April Fools. He was the child that would comfort her when she was down or not feeling well.

"It'll be okay, Mom," he would say.

From the time he was little, Tyler enjoyed sports. He played baseball, a game he loved. Other times he enjoyed fishing with his Grandpa. Then at thirteen, he took an interest in skateboarding.

Charlett was quick to point out that she resisted and discouraged Tyler from participating in skateboarding;

more so, due to the crowd so many associated with the sport. She understands now that the assumption skateboarders were all stoners and lowlifes was an overgeneralization of the group. Many of the youngsters simply loved skateboarding for what it represented-freedom and fun.

At the age of sixteen, Tyler was living in Idaho with his father. Charlett was living in California. One night at 2:00AM, she received a phone call that forever changed her life. She was told that Tyler had been riding in the back of a pickup truck. The driver, a good friend of his, reached for his cell phone and over-corrected. His truck moved up an embankment throwing Tyler from its bed and killing him instantly. The driver, Tyler's friend, was also killed.

Charlett described the pain of losing a child as the "most unimaginable thing she had ever felt." It was the type of pain that literally "brought her to her knees." To say that she was sickened and in shock when she received that call, and in the following days, would be an understatement.

She recalled looking around the room at those in attendance at Tyler's wake. The number of people he touched in his short life was astounding, and the lump she felt in her throat indigestible. Many of those listening as she talked about Tyler knew him at different stages in his life.

When I asked Charlett what motivated her to continue living, to sustain life as she knew it, her answer was clear and concise.

"My faith and my two other children," she replied.

When pressed, Charlett continued, "I've been told countless times my strength is amazing, but the truth is I didn't choose to be strong, I didn't choose to survive, but I chose to carry on for my children. I saw their pain. What would happen if they lost me too?"

As many do who search for answers after a sudden loss, Charlett turned to a spiritual medium. The lady she went to was a famous and very talented individual who claimed to speak with the dead and convey messages to loved ones. Many turn to mediums in hopes of contacting lost loved ones and bringing about a sense of closure, most especially when they are taken from us unexpectedly.

"Your son is talking to me about an event or fundraiser," she said to Charlett.

After Tyler's death, Charlett organized an annual skateboarding fundraiser at their previous home in Colorado. There was no doubt in her mind that the psychic medium was channeling Tyler and speaking to her through him. For a decade since Tyler's death, Charlett has organized the "Tear It Up For Tyler" skateboarding competition in Dorado, Colorado. It is there that she feels his presence and knows he is smiling upon his lovely mother and all the participants.

His spirit lives on in Charlett, and his memory is preserved at the skate park that he dreamed would be built prior to his death. When children cannot afford to enter the annual skateboarding competition, Charlett pays their entrance fee and feeds them hotdogs while they are there.

While many parents would lay down and refuse to get back up after the death of a child, Charlett perseveres and pushes forward. When I asked her how she did it, she provided the eulogy that she read at Tyler's funeral. Her strength and fortitude are amazing.

"I stand up here today, not because I want to but because I have to. I can tell you with absolute certainty that Tyler is up here with me right now. Just as he always did, he's holding me up and giving me the strength to do what I believe is impossible. He was a beautiful, inspiring young man whose life should be recognized. It took so long for me to find the words to use today but then I realized that no words will ever bring back Tyler or express to you how much I love and miss him.

"Tyler had one of the three most beautiful smiles I've ever known. The other two, of course, belong to his brother and sister. They will carry on without him, and their smiles will remind me of Tyler every day. From the moment he first smiled at me when he was a baby, I knew I'd live to see that smile for the rest of my life. I still see it-only now I have to close my eyes.

"Tyler was not just my son, he was my friend. He stood by me through anything, just as many of you have. He was loyal and devoted to those he loved. I never once saw him turn his back on someone he cared about. He stood up for me, defended me, and I always knew that Ty was one of my biggest fans. He didn't hold my mistakes against me, he just kept loving me. When you earned his love and respect, it was truly unconditional.

"A lot of you knew Tyler as a skater but there was so much more to him. His life can be defined in so many ways. He was a baseball pitcher, a basketball player, a fisherman, a snowboarder, a skateboarder, a comedian, a lady's man, a friend, a brother, a grandson, a cousin, a nephew, and a son. Not all of you were fortunate enough to know all of those parts of him but those of you that did know him, you know that he excelled at each and every one of them.

"Some of my favorite memories of Tyler were the trips we made to Six Flags together. He wasn't afraid of anything. I would always be nervous and scared when we were standing in line for the next roller coaster. He would always say, "come on mom, I'll be right beside you." And now, as I have to go on with my life, without him, I will have to believe that he meant those words. He went on all of the roller coasters over and over again. And when we walked by the bungee jumping booth, he looked at me and smiled. I looked back at him and said, NO WAY TYLER! Of course, his response was "Why not mom? That isn't so scary." And that was Tyler; the title of his life should read "No Fear".

"One song that I've thought of during this difficult time says that God only cries for the living, for we are the ones that have to carry on. We will all cry and mourn this tragic loss for a long time, but please remember that Tyler would want us to laugh.

"Every person has a reason and purpose on this earth. I believe that Tyler's purpose was to teach others how to live each day to its fullest, to live without fear, and to always pursue your dreams-one of his greatest qualities he took from his Uncle Darryl. He would never give up on something that he believed in. If he had to try over and over again to be successful, then that is what he did. Many times he was frustrated when learning a new skate trick but if it was something he wanted badly enough, he kept trying until he got it. He never worried about tomorrow but made certain he was living and laughing for today. We should take that lesson from Tyler as his gift to all of us.

"Tyler would want me to thank all of you for being part of his life, for making him laugh, making him smile, and sharing his dreams. You each played an important role in making him the person that he was. From the bottom of my broken heart, Tyler and I thank you."

According to the National Institute of Health, the loss of a child can bring about mental and physical ailments, unlike trauma of any sort. Many parents studied over time had shorter than expected lifecycles, as the bereavement period after losing a child was considerably longer than that of losing a different family member or loved one. As Charlett told us, the hole inside her can never be filled.

The loss of a child is every parent's worst nightmare. From the moment we hold our newborn in our arms, the concern a parent has for his or her child never wanes or wavers. The knock at the door, the ringing of a telephone, or the sad look on a doctor's face as he delivers the news—these are all things no parent wants to face.

Charlett was forced into this situation, and despite the grief she still feels, she has used the death of her son to promote something positive and holistically good in his memory. When participants show up to skateboard in the tournament, Charlett can feel Tyler there with her, smiling at those giving it their all on their boards, and at his mother who lives on in his absence. She gives reason and definition to the word "matriarch," for she is the pillar on which her family is built.

Brenda
Colorado

Brenda was young and full of life. Like many, she adored husband and children. One of those children was about to graduate from high school and the family was scheduled to take a trip to Hawaii to celebrate. Oddly, a few short months before the graduation ceremony and the flight over the Pacific, Brenda noticed an abnormality in one breast.

As she dressed for work each morning, she told herself it was nothing. The dreaded possibility of what the lump could be was covered by her clothing. Her work with an oil and gas exploration company kept her mind occupied and focused, but Brenda's family forced her attention on the oddity she had discovered.

Brenda called her doctor in October 2013 and the staff told her to come in immediately for a check-up, but she explained that her family had planned a trip to Hawaii and she could not miss it. The family had a wonderful trip; they celebrated their youngest daughter's high school graduation. In the back of her mind, however, she wondered how her life would change when she did see the doctor. Something gnawed at her, telling her the news would most likely be bad. Brenda's pessimistic outlook was typical of seeing a doctor for an abnormality.

On November 4, 2013, Brenda saw her doctor and had a mammogram performed. A short time later an ultrasound was ordered, followed by a biopsy. The technician who performed the biopsy told her that it didn't look good and that she would be called by 1:00PM the next day with the results.

"Don't be alone when you get the call," the technician advised Brenda.

Brenda was convinced she was sick, and at 10:00AM on November 6, 2013, she received the call telling her that she had invasive lobular breast cancer on her right breast. When the call came, she was alone.

Brenda recalled the beginning of her chemotherapy journey, "I met with the nurse assigned to my case who walked me through what the next year of my life would be like. It was a lot to take in and try to remember. Over the next week or two I met with a team of doctors, nutritionists, gene testing, surgeons, and oncologists. There were many decisions made in that first couple of weeks after diagnosis regarding my treatment. I elected to have a port put into my chest to allow for easy access each week for chemo treatments. The same day the port was put in I received my first chemo treatment. My first chemo treatment was on Wednesday, November 20th. The day after chemo I had to have a Neulasta shot. The shot was intended to help reduce the risk of infection during my treatments. It boosts the number of infection-fighting white blood cells, which help the immune system to strengthen. The shot itself wasn't difficult. What was to follow, however, was. The Neulasta caused my joints to hurt. I cannot begin to describe the pain. A few days after the first chemo treatment, my chest began hurting making it difficult to breath."

To say that she faced adversity head-on would not just be cliché, it would also be trite. Brenda met her mortality and stared it in the face. As with many dealing with life and death crises, she cherished each moment of every day. Time was significant and precious and she understood what it meant to live!

Pain became a constant in Brenda's life, just another side effect of the treatments she was forced to have. That said, there is a discernable difference between pain created from radiation and chemotherapy and that caused by the equipment used to allow the treatments to enter her fragile body.

She continued, "I can remember saying the port felt weird and caused me to breathe funny. I hurt all over and just assumed I needed to get used to the port. It was going to take time. The Sunday after my first chemo treatment, I spoke at a church youth group. My topic was *as daughters of God, we are stronger than we think we are.* I didn't know it at the time, but that would become my daily motto. During that talk I couldn't breathe very well, I kept coughing and struggling to catch my breath. The next day I decided I felt well enough to go to work…except for the whole breathing thing. I made it through the day, and that night the surgeon who inserted the port called to check on me. As soon as she heard my voice she told me I needed to get to the hospital immediately, and that she believed I had a hole in my lung…probably caused by the port. I spent the next 3 days in the hospital getting my lung inflated again. After my lung was healed, the port was no longer a concern and my breathing returned to normal. One of the things I learned during my treatment was to listen to my body, when it acts differently or feels differently do something about it."

I asked Brenda to describe her chemotherapy treatments and she responded, "I had sixteen chemo treatments; the first four were once a week every other Wednesday, followed by the Neulasta shot. The three days after chemo were the worst for me, because I hurt to the core. I spent those days in bed trying not to move. I could eat whatever I wanted, anything that I keep get down. I took anti-nausea medicine, and it worked well for me. My hair began falling out after the first treatment. It's crazy to lay your head down on a pillow only to get up and find it strew about. Running my hands through over my scalp led to having handfuls of hair.

"Losing my hair never bothered me. I thought it would, but a wonderful friend took me to a wig shop here in Denver whose owner was a breast cancer survivor. Before driving to the shop, I had my head shaved. I purchased a wig along with a few scarves. When a person is receiving chemo treatments their body is very sensitive, pores on the head hurt. Due to the sensitivity on my head and how hot the wig was, I was unable to wear it. I chose to wear scarves, which became kind of fun. I had one that matched everything I owned.

"I received my chemo treatments at the chemo center at Parker Hospital. It's a large room filled with recliners, IV drips, TV, magazines, and very caring nurses. The nurses at the center were absolutely amazing. They took care of me, and made me feel like the cancer was a bump in the road, or just a small hurdle to get over. They were always positive, informative, encouraging, and loving.

"One of the chemo meds I had to have was put directly into my port. It was red and came with a poison symbol on the bottle. The nurse who injected it into my port wore a gown, gloves, and mask. I told her there was something so wrong with that picture the first time I had it. She was completely protected from the stuff and was injecting it directly into my bloodstream. It was a little overwhelming

"I went to my treatments by myself and had panic attacks at a few treatments. I had very good friends that sent me texts and called during the treatment that helped me to get through the anxiety. After I finished four treatments of that drug, I was switched to chemo every Wednesday for the next twelve weeks. It was so overwhelming and daunting thinking about having chemo until April. April was so far away.

"The new drug was so much better than the previous drug, and I didn't need the Neulasta shot any longer. The new chemo drug caused my eyelashes and eyebrows to fall out. That was more difficult than losing my hair. I was able to work every day except Wednesdays when I had chemo. One of the drugs they gave me caused me to stake awake the first night, so I would lie around and watch movies. My last chemo treatment was April 2nd. I cried leaving the chemo room that day. The nurses and staff had become my family, my safe place. It was an emotional time, very happy to be done with treatment, but sad to have to leave that emotional support that I received every week.

"In May I chose to have a double mastectomy and a complete hysterectomy. The type of cancer I had would come back in the other breast, and I tested positive for the BRACA II gene which put me at a higher risk for ovarian cancer. On the same day, I also started reconstruction. It was a rough recovery, as the pain from the reconstruction was incredible.

"In July, I began a series of twenty-eight radiation treatments. Radiation was more of an inconvenience compared to the chemotherapy. I had to go every day Monday through Friday. By the time the treatments were finished my skin was pretty burned. My skin was raw in places, and getting dressed was painful. On August 1st I finished treatment and my cancer was considered in remission! Just as my last day after receiving my final chemo treatment, I cried leaving the cancer center. I was so happy to be finished, but leaving behind the support was hard."

After asking Brenda about her cancer and the incredible challenges facing her during chemotherapy and radiation, I wondered what her current life goals were and how she would achieve them.

"When I was diagnosed with cancer my life changed completely. My twenty-three year marriage ended, my youngest graduated from high school, and my children no longer needed me. I had a lot of trouble with the reconstruction process. After the implants were put in, I got an infection and had to have one removed. Six months later, I was able to have another reconstructive procedure. Once the healing from the reconstruction was complete, my final surgery was ordered. I felt as though my life was on hold for a couple of years. Every time I began to feel good, it would be time for another surgery and I was forced to begin the process over again. My life goal is to remain healthy, and to get my body as strong as it can be so if, and when, the cancer returns I can fight it with the same strength, sense of humor, and gusto I did the first time. I am in the process of redefining who I am. I attend charity events for cancer survivors, and want to help others facing this battle. So many women face this battle alone, and I want to help as many as I can."

I then asked what got her through everything she faced, from the time of the diagnosis, through treatment, to watching her marriage fall apart, and finally to recovery. Finally, I asked what she would say to someone else facing a similar challenge.

"When I was diagnosed, not fighting the disease was never an option. I knew I would do whatever necessary to preserve my life a little longer on this earth. I wanted to meet my grandchildren on this earth, not in heaven. Through my faith I know that this life is a test. It will be filled with trials and struggles. We learn and grow and become refined through hard challenges, sorrow, and difficult choices. Each of us will face dark days filled with pain, but without these challenges we would not know joy and love. Throughout my treatments, surgeries, and the pain that all of them brought, I never prayed for the cancer to be gone. I always asked my Heavenly Father to give me strength to get through it. He did. I truly know that I was never alone, but was carried through to the very end of my treatments. A dear friend sent me this scripture from Proverbs 31:25 not long after my initial diagnosis. 'She is clothed in strength and dignity and she laughs without fear of the future.' That scripture hangs on my wall today. I did everything that I could do, and I never want to look back.

"My advice (to those battling cancer) would be to keep your sense of humor! Find the good in every day, stay positive, motivated, and surround yourself with people and things that mean something to you. Make plans for the future, and continue to do the things you love as much as your body allows. Life changes forever when you are diagnosed with cancer. It may not seem like it, but your life will return to normal, not the normal you know, but a new normal. Not a day goes by that I do not think about the cancer. Will it come back? Can I beat it again? I do not dwell on it though. It is a passing thought that I put aside so that I may live life. Every time I look in the mirror I see scars and a very different body, but I am never sad about it. My scars are a part of me, the part that defines my strength, the part that helps me remember every day that I'm stronger than I think I am. It is the part that reminds me that every day is a gift, and a blessing. Treasure those you love and enjoy every day."

Facing your own mortality is an inevitability we must all come to terms with at some point in our lives. That said, to face it head on in your early forties when the world is at your fingertips is something most cringe at, or refuse to consider altogether. Brenda was forced into that position and dealt with it with the courage of a lion.

To say that she has suffered and lost would be an understatement, but anyone reading her story will understand how valiant and inspirational she is. Many people would have given up when told of the cancer, or laid around crying when their hair fell out. Others would never recover from losing a spouse who should have been there throughout the entire ordeal. Brenda not only survived, but thrives, which makes her more than remarkable.

Psychologists T.F. Hack and L.F. Degner stated that women diagnosed with breast cancer and faced their diagnosis head on fared much better than those who pretended they never received the news from their respective doctors, or reacted poorly as a result of receiving the diagnosis. Hack and Degner surmised that women who became depressed at the time of their diagnosis continued to be depressed and mentally weary three years after receiving the news. Those women who coped with the disease and chose to fight it head-on tended to be in a much better frame of mind over the course of the same timeframe.

Brenda is LIVING proof that an unyielding faith in God, a positive attitude, and a "never say die" attitude can help propel anyone in the right direction. Today, she lives not in fear of the cancer returning, but with hope, resilience, and a lust for life with friends and family!

Brian
Illinois

My friend Brian is a fascinating individual—head-strong, independent, and a devoted husband and father. You may be thinking, "That is not so out of the ordinary," and you would be right, except you probably have never met this man. What makes Brian so unique is his extraordinary story.

"I was born and raised on the south side of Chicago by two blue-collar, old school parents. I am of Irish descent and raised in the Catholic Church. I have two sisters, one two years older than me, and one four years younger. I went to parochial grammar and high schools taught by nuns and the Christian Brothers of Ireland. As a kid, I played every sport available and had a job when I was fifteen years old. Acquiring a good education was important to my parents, and as a result, I am a first generation college graduate in my family.

"On a chilly day after Christmas 1979, at the age of seventeen, I broke my neck while playing football with my friends. I found the courage and strength to recover, graduate from high school, earn a college degree, and earn my Juris Doctor degree from DePaul College of Law as a quadriplegic. I also continued with hours of therapy a day while obtaining my education."

Brian explained to me that while in college he played wheelchair rugby and started coaching football at a local grammar school. It was at that time he says he found his purpose—to achieve more than anyone expected of him!

Being the best at whatever he put his mind to was his sole aspiration.

After graduating from law school, Brian worked at a local law firm for years before transitioning into sales and management for a Fortune 500 company. He said, "I had work longer and harder than others to earn the opportunities I wanted."

At twenty-seven, Brian married his sweetheart he met while in law school. "We bought a house and got a dog, then tried to start our family, but were unsuccessful. After numerous unsuccessful artificial inseminations, my wife and I decided to adopt. I am the father of three fantastic kids and a husband of over 27 years."

"I love the outdoors and coached football and basketball over twenty years. I am also a certified John Maxwell trainer and speaker. Last year I started a nonprofit called SOAR: Swift Outdoor Accessible Recreation*. SOAR is dedicated to helping people with disabilities participate in outdoor recreational activities such as camping, fishing, hiking, hunting, four wheeling, bicycling, and more."

Brian explained that individuals suffering from spinal cord injuries resulting in paralysis often fixate, in many cases understandably so, on their lack of mobility and reliance on others to function on a day-to-day basis. Beyond depression and the internal mental war one must face when confined to a wheel chair, the physical issues he or she is forced to deal with are many: bladder and bowel control; sexual functionality; pain at the point of injury, or phantom pains (real pain in the area of an injury, despite having no physical sensation at that specific point); tingling sensations; gastrointestinal problems; difficulty breathing; and on-going skin issues such as bed sores if the person is not active.

At one point, I asked Brian about depression and whether he had suffered from its effects. His response was interesting and not what I expected.

"Yes I have dealt with depression but not until many years later, about twenty, after my injury. Remember whether you're walking or wheeling you will get knocked down, you will have major disappointments and frustrations in your life so you can't always blame your condition. I was too busy living to let depression get a big hold on me. My down time, as I called it, never lasted long.

"Find something constructive and positive that helps you cope with your mental and physical pain. Do not cop out (and begin) using marijuana, prescription drugs, or alcohol. You are better than that. Your mind, heart, and mettle will get you through those difficult times."

Like the other contributors to this work, I asked Brian what motivated him to push forward. His responses, just like the man himself, were direct, succinct, and clear.

"As a quadriplegic, my faith gets tested daily or even hourly. The strength of my faith comes from my mom. Both of my parents have never faltered in their faith—in me, nor in God. My faith has continued to grow over the years as I learn more about myself, The Bible, and my responsibility as the man of my house and the example I must be to my family.

"Fear is also a tremendous motivator. The fear of not succeeding at something or in life haunts me. Even though I come from very modest parents and (and even more modest) lifestyle, I have high expectations for myself. I also have high expectations for my family, the people I mentor, as well as those I coach. Being a C 5 Quadriplegic has not changed that. Actually, it has increased my desire to prove, to myself and to everyone that I could be successful and beat the statistics and expectations.

"My family is a tremendous motivation for me! There is nothing stronger than what family can do for each other. I am blessed to have my mom and dad involved in my life and in my family's life. They have been unbelievable examples of love, support, commitment, integrity attitude, and faith. With support and faith like this in my life, I had no choice but to succeed.

"Lastly, I have a strong passion for life. Life is fantastic, but only if you make the best of it. You will get out of it what you put into it, and walking is not necessarily a prerequisite for happiness. I have experienced more, failed, and succeeded at more than many people who walk could ever imagine. I have peed my pants and crapped myself in boardrooms and bars. Once you get over stuff like that, you realize that most of the noise and fear we put in our minds is nonsense. My trinity of FAITH, FAMILY, and FRIENDS really help drive my passion for life."

Brian is an inspiration to everyone forced to deal with obstacles and misfortune in life. What might cause others to fall into depression or self-pity only makes him want to be stronger and his life more valuable to those around him. Imagine, if you can, being a vibrant seventeen year old with your life ahead of you, then suddenly everything you have known and understood in the world is changed. You can no longer walk, run, or even stand. How would you face tomorrow if this were your plight?

His faith, family, and circle of friends are his motivation for a life well lived. In his mind, there is no disability, only a challenge set before him to overcome. Naturally, he still hopes and prays for a cure to his paralysis and desires to walk again, but if it does not happen in his lifetime, Brian is quick to point out that his life has been full and rich.

Along with his SOAR* (www.soarnonprofit.com), Brian has authored and co-authored several books including, <u>Up: Getting Up is the Key to Life</u>, <u>The Unofficial Guide to Fatherhood</u>, and <u>Go Ask Your Dad: Questions, Answers, & Stories About Fathers, Fatherhood & Parenting</u>.

Smith
Alabama

In 1970, a young man (who asked that he remain nameless) joined the United States Marine Corps. Many of his friends would consider him crazy, reckless, and perhaps a little suicidal to volunteer for the military at the height of the Vietnam War. With so many Americans drafted into the armed forces, Smith felt it was his duty to heed his country's call and fight for freedom in the jungles of Vietnam and did so without Uncle Sam making a personal request.

Lance Corporal Smith trudged through dense vegetation, over mountainous terrain, and through swamps on point while walking point for his unit. He described having to share a two-man tent with ten soldiers. The unit grew close and each man was willing to give his life for the other.

While walking through the tough topography in southeastern Asia, Smith personally witnessed things no man or woman would ever desire to see. Young children used to attack and kill soldiers, sometimes strapped with bombs were periodic reminders of how different and desperate their enemy was. Smith talked of hunting his enemy and killing him, but the most damning and life altering came when he was "in country" around the six month mark.

He explained to me, "(I) saw, heard, touched, (and) carried my fellow Marines to helicopters for evacuation. Many were wounded, some were dead. I carried a leg and hip of a fallen brother because that was all that was left of him. I did that so his family could at least bury what was left of his remains.

"Often, I was hungry, thirsty, infested with bugs, muddy, and wet. Two to four hours of sleep was a blessing, but rarely occurred. I was twice wounded, and sent home after losing an eye. I cannot imagine what the men and women who were there for a full year, or more, went through.

"I don't want anyone to think I'm complaining or sorry—I volunteered to go to Vietnam, joined, and was accepted into the Marine Corps. Knowing what I know now would have no bearing on my decision to do it all again," he finished.

Smith has suffered from what used to be known as "shell shock," now formally PTSD, or *post-traumatic stress disorder*. The condition comes in different forms, but ultimately the impact on the human psyche is beyond significant. I asked to detail his own PTSD experiences.

"I'm hyper vigilant and always expect violence anytime I leave my house. I trusted no one above the rank of sergeant (and still struggle to trust today)," he stated.

Smith discussed the problem he had controlling his anger, telling me he would often take things out on his wife and children. After a moment of reflection he said, "To this day, I don't understand what or why I was mad. Therapists, psychiatrists, and doctors gave me their educated opinions, but they all sounded like rubbish to me because none of them knew (anything) about combat."

He went on to tell me that unexplained noises have "sent me to the floor. Loud, unexpected voices, pops, bangs would trigger a 'startle reflex.' Walking through the woods and seeing a spider web strung between trees sent me back in time, as my memories were flooded with images of trip wires and explosives."

Smith told me that he now takes medication to control some of the anxiety that periodically crops up. "In my younger years, taking a pill was a sign of weakness, primarily because the pills I take prohibited me from responding and solving any and all threats I may encounter in my daily routine."

Along with the aforementioned PTSD concerns were also the nightmares. Smith stated that he drank heavily when he returned home from Vietnam, but eventually quit because alcohol would often intensify his dreams. Coupled with his anger and trust issues, drinking would only intensify his problems.

At the end of his interview, Smith told me as explicitly as he could, "...I remember some of the VC (Viet Cong: I.E. northern Vietnamese Army) that got away because I could not shoot all of them. I would have to reload, and too many of them were running in different directions. I wish I could have killed them all. Maybe if I could have shot 'that one,' another American would have come home alive."

He detailed for me his need for faith and family that pulled him through the darkest of times. Without each, and without the patience of his wife, Smith is not sure where he would have wound up or what his life would have become. What he does know is that his God and his family have made life bearable.

In 2011, Smith's wife and son arranged a trip to Washington D.C. where he visited the Vietnam Memorial for the first and only time of his life. It was there that he found some solace and peace and it was at The Wall that he left an engraved acrylic rock with a poem his wife had given him. He changed the words on the inscription in remembrance of his fallen brothers.

"We Are the Willing,
Led by the Qualified
To Do the Necessary
For the Ungrateful"

Only soldiers who have fought and come home understand the perils of war. Some killed and lived with the aftermath, and some were seriously injured and are reminded daily of their time spent in combat. Smith lost an eye in Vietnam, but to say he lost much more would be an understatement. Coping with the ghosts of our past is difficult and complicated in the best of times, but consider for a moment that those spirits give you no reprieve or rest and insist on visiting you even while you sleep.

Post-Traumatic Stress Disorder can be, and is, triggered by serious events outside our normal routine. Sudden death, accidents, and other life altering happenings stick in a person's mind, dominates their thoughts, and sometimes impedes their actions. This said, I do believe that PTSD acquired during wartime is succinctly different from its non-combat related brethren. The constant stress, possibly witnessing death on multiple occasions, inflicting death on others, the worry of bombs, grenades, gunfire, etc. coming at you without notice is different than a single event that leaves a stain in your mind.

It has been well documented that every day, on average, twenty-two veterans commit suicide. A strong support system is instrumental for the returning warrior as he transitions from soldier to citizen. Most do not ask for pity or sympathy and try to cope with the mental wounds inflicted upon them when they served for our country. Additionally, self-medicating is a consistent theme for many dealing with the effects of PTSD.

Identifying the problems that plague our veterans and helping them regain a foothold in their new reality should be priority number one for each of us. Let not the opportunity to extend a helping hand to an American hero pass.

Melissa
Florida

Coping with the death of a very close friend is as traumatic as losing a family member. The relationships we develop over a lifetime help shape our personalities, define who we are, and in a strange way, who we become. Humans have a way of connecting with others quite unlike the animals that roam the planet. There are the emotional, interpersonal, deeply seeded relationships that we are capable of developing in a very short amount of time that take root, and with the right amount of attention, blossom into a mutual feeling that cannot be undone by anyone or anything.

Jonathan and Melissa grew to be good friends in high school. As she told me, "He and I were class clowns back then. Impish, and stubborn, we lived life as if we were immortal. Jonathan was somewhat oafish and lumbering, and always self-deprecating in his humor." He also told his friends that he was born with an underdeveloped heart.

As with many, or even most high school friends, life took them in different directions. Jonathan married and had children, as did Melissa once she completed her undergraduate degree. As though by some mystical force, the two rekindled their friendship after Jonathan's divorce. As was typical of the two, they decided to go to their high school reunion as "dates."

Over the years, they would attend high school reunions together. Melissa told me about one such event when Jonathan brought an electronic vaping cigarette with him.

He stuffed it in his sports jacket pocket and the two set off in search of misadventure and a good time. A short time later, the e-cigarette caught fire causing Jonathan to remove the jacket and throw it on the floor. They all watched as his jacket burned, and had a good laugh, most especially since no one was hurt during the ordeal.

Melissa went on to explain their extraordinary friendship. "There are times in life that are uneventful, and then there were the times I spent with Jonathan. He thought I was the coolest chick on the face of the Earth. Being around him almost made me feel like I was. I came to understand my role in his life was to make him feel better. Never was I sure exactly what ailed him, but I always ready for a comedy routine with a captive audience, no matter if the audience was just one. Our lunch visits were as common as our nighttime shenanigans. I looked forward to being with him."

We often hear about friends, or have experienced it ourselves, that 'pick up right where they left off' after not speaking for several years. This was Melissa and Jonathan. Their story reminded me of Forrest Gump's famous line when Jenny came back into his life, "We were just like peas and carrots." The two of them just 'went' together.

Over lunch, the two would plan their daytime television show they wanted to host. Melissa would be the sports analyst and Jonathan would be the fashion and reality television show analyst. Along with their daytime television plans, the two would sometimes discuss how they would be roommates in a nursing home once they grew old. Jonathan would look at Melissa and remind her of his underdeveloped heart then say, "I never planned on getting old. Don't forget."

Melissa was intimately aware of Jonathan's personal struggles, but as she confided, "He never complained. Never. Ever."

Besides his heart ailment, her best friend suffered from diabetes-like symptoms, although he was never diagnosed with the disease. Some of the symptoms included forgetfulness, slurring of words, and other similar issues that made him appear drunk. He battled other demons, and coupled with a desire to mask it all with alcohol, Jonathan's life was in a precarious place.

When he was at his lowest point, as desperate as a person could be, he met a young woman—Kitty. She was the yin to his yang. A noticeable difference in his personality appeared and just like that, he was full of spunk and vitality. The couple planned on moving in with one another and beginning a life together.

Sometimes Melissa and her husband would go on double dates with Jonathan and Kitty. They would meet for lunch or go to supper together. Wine and alcohol were generally part of the mix. Melissa and Jonathan would have spirited political debates, she of the liberal ilk and he of the conservative persuasion.

Jonathan and Kitty bought a house together, purchased a new car, and best of all, he received a job offer. He was to reenter the workforce after a long drought and was excited to do so. With the good news came more reason to celebrate, and with celebration came more reason to drink.

I asked Melissa about Jonathan's drinking problem and she told me that, "Even I had no clue how bad it was. [All I knew was that] Kitty made him want to be the best he could be. He thought he had time to kick the habit before he started his new job."

In March of 2016, Melissa contracted the flu. Shortly after getting sick, she received a call from Kitty telling her Jonathan had been admitted to the hospital. Since she was contagious, Melissa decided it was best to stay away from the hospital to avoid contaminating anyone else with the virus. After a week, she made her way to the hospital to visit her friend.

"He looked awful, but as I glanced from him to Kitty, I quickly assessed they did not find the situation to be as dire as I. She was with him daily. He was hooked up to a few IVs, but they both assured me he would be fine. Perhaps some drainage, surgery, or a pill will fix this. I had no idea of the diagnosis, but both of them seemed like it was a typical Sunday afternoon, with each them with their faces in books and newspapers. I would visit him often after that. I brought him some porn magazines I bought at a gas station. The issues were classics from the 1970's, so we had a great time laughing at all the...articles. Then, he threw me the curveball of all curveballs.

"My liver is failing, Mis..."

Jonathan told Melissa that privately. Kitty was unaware of the diagnosis, and undoubtedly not aware of the prognosis. He did not have the heart to tell his soul mate the news, so it fell to Melissa to deliver it.

"The eternal optimist, born from a flower, raised by unicorns, Kitty is someone who always sees the positive, but staying in the hospital day-in-and-day-out was wearing on her. The smiles were slower to grace her beautiful face, and she wore her worry almost as visibly as she wore her shoes. One day after a particularly long night, I had to break the news to her that her beloved was dying," Melissa confided.

Melissa received a text in the early hours of April 16, 2016 that Jonathan had taken a turn for the worst. She drove to the hospital, walked into his room, and knew right then he was not long for the world.

"His gasps grew fewer and our tears more plentiful. We were all exhausted and finally moved to accept the inevitable. There was nothing else to do but watch, pray, and talk to him. I held onto his foot and big toe because I am the epitome of awkward in tough situations. Then, just like that, my best friend died.

"After the anger was the numbness stage. I would like the numbness stage added to the usual denial, bargaining, etc., because it most definitely exists. I know that, just as it did after my father's death, time will ease my pain. My loss should be, at some point, less profound, but as I sit here ten months into my life without Jonathan, I still understand that I am not over his death. My first priority after he died was making sure his Kitty was cared for. Kitty and I still have our crying sessions, but we have since developed a closer bond than I ever knew could have existed. Some days I help her cope, and some days she helps me. Jonathan brought us together, almost foreseeing the void he would leave. I am still reminded of the cruel but comforting circle of life. As sure as the sun rises, it sets.

Now, I carry with me a sense of pride when I think of Jonathan. I was a good friend to him, up until the end. I always look back on tragic events in my life and am humbled by my strength, surprised at my resiliency, touched by my hope. Jonathan taught me that tomorrow is never guaranteed, and to treat people kindly. Oh, and he taught me to laugh."

Melissa's story is not an uncommon one on the surface, but the friendship she shared with Jonathan was a close, mutually respectful one that many people struggle to find in life. Such friendships are remarkably difficult to find, and the pain felt when one of the friends passes from this life can be as intense and woeful as losing a close family member.

As important as their friendship, has been the incredible way Melissa has treated Jonathan's passing; she has done so with grace, love, and beautiful memories for him and his love, Kitty. The struggles of losing someone so close can lead to guilt, depression, and anguish, but as much as Melissa has borne these feelings, she was also desperate to tell her story.

To her, and for her, Jonathan was more than family; he was a kind, gentle friend who did not pass judgment on her. For Melissa, his life and memories are to be cherished. Such should it be for those left behind after our loved ones pass over.

Irene
Alabama

May 12, 2011

"Everyone urged me to write down my experiences during the tornado on that fateful day. They said it would be "therapeutic" for me and that it will help me to "remember." I don't know if it is therapeutic, and I don't think that I will ever forget, but it is hard for me to keep retelling the story to well-meaning friends, so maybe this will help explain.

"We knew the entire day of April 27th that severe weather was expected (including tornadoes). I worked at a local bank in Tuscaloosa, Alabama, and it closed at noon that day for our safety. Everyone went home but me, as I had an appointment with a customer. I finished up with my customer around 1:00 PM and prepared to leave the office. My friend and co-worker, Jennifer had come back to the bank at that time and told me that she, her mother, and her son were going to "ride out the storm" at the office. They asked me to stay with them but I was anxious to get home.

"I stopped off at a gas station on my way home to get my "tornado supplies" – a Mountain Dew and three packs of cigarettes! I called my friend Ginger and laughingly told her I was ready for the storm. I was so arrogant, although I did not recognize it at the time.

"I got home and changed into my comfiest pajamas and was puttering around on the computer – I had a local station touting the seriousness of the storms on the television, but I honestly was not paying much attention. Tornado sirens went off a few times, but again I thought it was for "rural" Tuscaloosa and trailer parks, and that it would never hit Central Tuscaloosa. I paid them no mind.

"I am not sure of the time, but somewhere between two and three P.M., my Dad called me from Jasper and said I needed to get in a safe place—there was a tornado headed my way! I assured him I would, but continued playing on the computer.

"Between four and five in the afternoon, my friend Jane called from Birmingham and said there was a really bad tornado on TV and was headed straight for me! I went into my den and watched the tornado on the television and then realized that the tornado on the screen was bearing down on my home! From the back door I could see transformers exploding, and I knew from my hurricane experiences on the Gulf of Mexico that seeing the arc flash as they blew up was not a good sign. As if in slow motion, everything outside started swirling and my ears began to pop as the air pressure around me dropped.

"When I say one minute saved my life, I am not exaggerating. I turned and darted into the bathroom, shut the door, and sat down on the side of the tub just as the tornado hit the back of my house. The back wall must have received the full brunt of the storm, as the den where I had been standing was no longer there. It was obliterated along with both bedrooms, the dining and living room.

"The next few moments are still a bit blurry, and I am still trying to piece it all together, but I know my ears continued to pop. I remember the sound of the tornado hitting my house, and it sounded as though I was being bombed (by the way, it did not sound like a freight train, it sounded like an explosion). I heard glass breaking everywhere, and I remember the house shaking and moving. For some time, I thought my shower doors fell on me in, but soon learned what hit me was actually the wall coming down. I know the mirror in the bathroom shattered and I can remember glass and debris hitting me in the face. While I covered my head and eyes, I was being pelted by several objects – sheetrock, bricks, glass, and everything on the bathroom counter. I remember hearing the roof being ripped from the trusses, and then suddenly feeling my body being pulled up into the storm along with the house!

"I held onto the barrier wall with everything I had, but had no doubt I was going to die. At that moment, in what I thought were my last moments of my life, nothing mattered but for me to tell my family how much I loved them, but also realized I had no way of telling them.

"I lost track of time and do not know if it took a minute, an hour, or a day for the storm to pass. At one point it seemed to get a little bit calmer and I thought that perhaps it was over, but felt my stomach sink when it began again. I don't know if a tornado is like a hurricane when the eye passes over, but I do know I got took another direct hit as it continued to pass over what was left of my home.

"There was a sudden stillness, but I could still feel and hear the wind and the noise from beyond. I do not recall how long I was in the bathroom, but eventually I heard someone at the door ask if anyone was inside, I could not speak. For once in my life, my big mouth would not work.

"I heard the person leaving before managing to yell, 'I am here!'

"The person or people beyond my bathroom door tried to get in, but the door was jammed and they could not open it.

"The voice, a man's voice screamed at me, 'I'll be back!'

"I thought to myself, 'No you won't. You are just going to leave me here for dead.'

"At long last, one of my neighbors did come back with more people, and they were able to get the door open just a crack. When they finally pulled me from the rubble, I saw that my house was gone. I was literally standing outside–and nothing remained. The roof, walls, furniture—everything was gone!

"People carried me out of what remained of my home. The wood, sheetrock, and bricks from the outer wall had fallen on my legs. My ability to walk was very limited. One of my neighbors, a nursing student, examined me and said I needed to get to a hospital as soon as possible. She later told me that my leg had no pulse and feared I would lose it.

"I raised my head and quickly realized every home on my street had been leveled. The smell of natural gas wafted over the open air, and live power lines lay strewn about, just daring someone to touch them.

"As I mentioned before, I had on flip-flops and pajamas, and sat there in shock, soaked from the rain after the tornado passed.

"My neighbors carried me to the corner of my block, as there was no way for an ambulance to navigate through the debris field. They sat me on the curb and found a trash can to elevate my leg before leaving me in order to find help. They located a police officer and he found a vehicle to take me to the hospital. Unfortunately, the car had flat tires that had to be changed before it could be driven.

"Straight away, rumors began circulating that another tornado was headed our way. I watched as people were walked around aimlessly trying to get to some sort of shelter, but there was nothing left to cover them. It was like watching an apocalyptic movie where people just wandered around with a vacant look in their eyes, while carrying what few possessions they could salvage.

"The men got the tires changed, and a neighbor was able to move trees from the street so I could get to a local hospital. Most roads were impassable, but we managed to dodge electrical wires, trees, and remnants of homes. I could not believe what I was seeing. Nothing looked the same as it had a few hours earlier. Landmarks were gone, buildings gone, cars flipped and strewn everywhere. What remained of my hometown looked eerily like a war-torn country that you see on the evening news.

"When we arrived at the hospital, it was all, if you will pardon my cliché, surreal–I still cannot get those sights and sounds out of my head. There were people everywhere, some hurt badly, and there were calls for crash carts continually with no power in the hospital. Triage stations were set up in the cafeteria, while all the employees, medical staff, and volunteers were running around tending to the injured. The thing I remember most is that with all those injured people, no one was moaning, screaming, or yelling; everyone was quiet. I assumed we were all in shock, but as I think back on that night, I am sure there was a strange sense of unity and community that precluded complaining.

"I have never felt as alone as I did that night. I could not reach anyone on my phone, nor could anyone call me. Cell towers in the surrounding area had been destroyed, and the few that remained were overloaded. I naturally assumed everyone thought I had been killed in the storm.

"Finally, a few calls started coming in and I was able through to my parents' neighbor. I asked her to tell my parents what happened and that I was okay, but still in the hospital. My parents told her to tell me that they were on their way. To this day, I still do not know how they were able to get through, as the tornado had also affected them and all the roads leading into Tuscaloosa. Amazingly, I was able to get onto social media and communicate with my brother who lived in California and was frantic to hear any news of us.

"I noticed a little girl, she was maybe four years old, on a stretcher close to me, and she was crying quietly. I asked the nurse what was wrong and she told me they could not find the little girl's mother or grandmother...I asked the nurse to put her on the bed with me. She and I just held onto each other, happy for the moment that we had one another to comfort.

"When my parents arrived at the hospital, I saw them and let go of every emotion I had contained since the tornado stuck my house. We all cried.

"After a lot of reflection and consideration, I realized I lost my home, my car, and all my material things, but I was alive and I was blessed. I had insurance, I had a job, and I continue to have a lot of people who care about me!

"I will be okay, and Tuscaloosa will be okay.

April 27, 2012

"At the one year anniversary mark of the devastating tornado that changed our lives, I reflected on everything that transpired. I attempted to put things in perspective and continue to give thanks for everything I still have. It feels like I am an entirely different person than I was on that fate-filled day.

"I continue to have so many conflicting emotions. I am sad for the lives and property lost, but grateful that my life was spared. I sometimes feel guilty that I am alive, blessed that I had the resources that others did not, and happy with my new life. Yes, I am impatient that Tuscaloosa still has so far to go to rebuild, and worried that it could happen again, but as the crews did with the debris after the storm, we each pick up the pieces and move on with our respective lives.

"I still have nightmares, although not as frequently, but I do not believe there is a day that goes by that I do not think of that day. I know that who I am now has been determined by that storm-ravaged day, and know I am strong. There are times I still feel that lost, sick, helpless feeling and pray that diminishes as the days, months, and years go by.

"I have the best family and friends anywhere and I appreciate them so much more, and do not take things for granted like I did prior to that day.

"I am proud of our community and our state for what we have accomplished. What we have done has been remarkable. The way we all came together, the volunteers, the way we did not wait for the government to come "fix it." We jumped into the fray with our chain saws, our pick-up trucks, and our hands and went to work immediately.

"I thank everyone whose names I do not or cannot recall that were there with axes, gloves, bottles of water, a sandwich, a kind word or a prayer that helped me and others who were impacted. God knows who you are!

"To all my family and friends who came to dig through the rubble to try and salvage anything, my most heartfelt thank you is yours to bear. I thank my co-workers who raised money and sent me care packages of clothes and toiletries. To need even the most basic of necessities can be harrowing, and my angels came to the rescue."

Irene touched on something that should be explored, even from a top level. Survivor's guilt or remorse is a genuine thing for those who left to live after a traumatic event. It is closely related to post-traumatic stress disorder (PTSD) according to leading psychologist and psychiatrists, but there are two distinct and interesting elements.

Survivors of war, accidents resulting in the death of others, violence, and yes, natural disasters each deal with the sparing of their own life in unique ways. For some, feelings of guilt flourish until such time has passed that the individual suffering from the feelings of guilt can process what happened and come to grips with the fact that he or she was allowed to live.

Survivor's Guilt can be quantified into two camps: rational and irrational. An example of rational survivor's grief can be seen from a soldier's perspective. A unit comes under fire, and one soldier is careful as he advances toward the enemy. His buddy is not so careful and is shot and killed. The soldier who lived feels guilty for the loss of his friend, and wonder's what he could have done to prevent it from happening. After time passes, he realizes the lost soldier died as a result of his own carelessness.

On the other hand, as in Irene's case, feelings of guilt abound after natural disasters, most especially when some lives are lost and others left to live another day. Wondering how or why she survived while others were taken is both natural and irrational. Irrational, in this case, does not mean irresponsible or without merit; on the contrary, the mind does not understand how to cope with a random act such as a natural disaster, nor does it initially process the how or why something like a tornado spared her while killing others.

Survivor's guilt can be very difficult for others to comprehend. Empathy and openness for the person suffering from it should be given, rather than ignoring the individual. Irene's story and subsequent emotions are authentic, and help can be given to survivors by reaching out to grief counselors and close friends who do not shun such feelings.

Finally, I find her story captivating and inspirational. Her ability to overcome so much personal loss, rebound wholly and completely, and continue to flourish should be something we celebrate as a species.

Lee Ann
Wyoming/Georgia

We all have stories to tell, some more heart wrenching than others, but few times in my life have I heard of one like Lee Ann's. To say she is an inspiration to everyone who knows her is to marginalize what she has faced. In my opinion, if anyone were to justify giving up on life, it would have been her, but the indelible human spirit thrives deep within her soul.

Depression, addiction, sickness, financial ruin—she has faced it all, and when lesser people would have given up, she has pushed forward and pressed on with her life. The loss of a child, as we have already read, can be life altering. It is unnatural in life, yet all too frequent, or at least it would seem. The loss of two children, divorce, a husband dealing with a deadly form of cancer, and financial woes is the stuff we see scripted in Hollywood and watch come to life on the silver screen. Few of us know of anyone dealing with multiple hardships, but Lee Ann's story, while full of despair and pain is also one of hope, faith, and a strength we all strive to acquire.

This is her story. I encourage you to drink it in, contemplate her struggles, and ask yourself how you would handle the catastrophes life has dealt her.

Lee Ann grew up in a large family in Wyoming. She was the oldest of four girls, and also had two older brothers. As she explains, "I had a very loving family and knew I, too, wanted a big family someday." Her parents and siblings made a very loving home; this is how she understood a family should work.

Like many teenagers, Lee Ann's last two years of high school were times of freedom, freedom of expression, and a time to explore her sexuality. She quickly learned that she was pregnant not long after she graduated and had to face her parents with the truth. As most parents are not when they learn of their adolescent children's indiscretions, they weren't exactly thrilled with the news.

In 1986, at the age of nineteen, Lee Ann gave birth to her first child. As she relayed to me, "After hours of labor, a nurse placed the most beautiful baby on my chest. I knew for the first time in my life what absolute, unconditional love was. I felt as though I had been waiting for him my whole life, and God had chosen this little boy just for me.

"I think my mom stayed the entire night, sitting in a chair, next to my bed holding Michael the whole time. She was as in love with him as I was. The next day Michael and I went home to my parents' house where he was loved immediately by everyone."

Like many young couples, Lee Ann and her then boyfriend struggled to maintain a healthy relationship, despite the love both felt for their son. He had moved out of state during her pregnancy, but moved back shortly after Michael's birth. Their relationship seemed to be on track and growing healthier each day and when Michael was six months old, Lee Ann and her fiancé married.

Unfortunately, it was not long until things once again turned sour in the relationship. Sometimes things, as Lee Ann described them, would be very, very good, and at other times terrible. Arguing and the stress of being young parents, as many of us know, can take a toll on a relationship.

Despite the rocky nature of their marriage, they decided they wanted another child, as their experiences as parents were something both of them loved and enjoyed.

Two years and eight months after Michael was born, a younger brother, Jesse came into the world. Afterward, they had a third son, Matthew. Michael, the oldest brother, loved his younger siblings as only an older brother could.

Lee Anny's marriage, after ten turbulent years, ended. Just prior to their marriage ending, she acquired her real estate license and tried her hand at selling property to would be buyers in a town forty miles from their home. The boys were aged ten, seven, and four. Lee Ann moved her family as she embarked on her new career, but had no idea how difficult it would be for Michael.

Struggling with his parent's fighting and eventual divorce, Michael told his mom that he wanted to live with his father, as the move was too much. He was also unhappy that his mom had later begun dating Don, a building contractor she met through the real estate office. A sense of unraveling overcame Lee Ann; the thought of her son moving away left her with a huge void that could not be filled.

Lee Ann continued dating Don, who also had three sons form a previous marriage. His children were older than Lee Ann's, and both parents struggled with how discipline was to be carried out on the other's kids. As any couple in love is apt to do, they worked through their differences and soon found that co-parenting was doable. Also, Lee Ann's desire to have a large family continued when she and Don discovered she was pregnant with another son.

Michael loved his new little brother and proudly walked around with him sitting upon his shoulders. There was never any doubt with how Michael felt about his siblings; he loved them all. Even when they would fight and argue as brothers do, it was obvious to everyone how much he loved them.

Lee Ann explained that Michael made a few moves from his dad's house to hers before finally settling in with his father for good. Sometime later, he was found using marijuana and law enforcement became involved. She watched her son being led away in handcuffs, and when his court date arrived, the judge sentenced him to thirty days.

She asked the judge to allow them some leeway being letting Michael spend his thirty days in a rehabilitation center, rather than in the county jail. The judge agreed, and Michael was scheduled to check in and begin counseling.

As Lee Ann told me, "The facility that we found seemed as if it was going to be the perfect fit for Michael. He would be getting one-on-one counseling, as well as group and family sessions. I was extremely happy with what I thought was going to be a new beginning. Once again, though, I had to say goodbye to my son. He was angry and scared, and I was devastated. I think I cried the whole hour and a half drive home but, in my heart, I knew it was for the best. Unfortunately, it would turn out to be a huge mistake.

"The first thing they did was put him on two different antidepressants, one in the morning and one at night. The nighttime medication was used to calm him down because the morning medication made him antsy. After the fact, I found out that they did this to every child that was there, whether they were there for drugs, alcohol, depression, eating disorders, or any other condition. They were all put on antidepressants, and because Michael wasn't living in my home, the doctor that was prescribing the medications would not talk to me about my concerns.

"Michael loved his counselor and quickly formed a bond with her. We went once a week for group/family therapy, and I tried to go at least one more time during the week to visit him. I took the classes they recommended for the parents and could see the progress he was making. Our relationship was amazing except when we had the family sessions. They were difficult, to say the least. Aside from the fact that they were in a group setting it was me, my husband and Michael's dad, and stepmother. His feelings that came out during those sessions were devastating, but we were making progress and I felt certain that he was going to leave there in a much better state of mind. He asked to stay an extra week because his therapist had taken a week of vacation. Michael wanted one more week with her before he left, so he stayed the extra week, and then came home.

"I drove down and picked him up in July. He had a roommate at the clinic who listened to classical music and Michael had learned to love it. We listened to Mozart and talked all the way home. It was a very special day that I often reflect upon. Aside from some horrible side effects (from the antidepressants), he was doing amazingly well. I planned on making an appointment with his primary care doctor to talk about the medications he was taking and see if we could do something about changing some of them, or perhaps the dosages, or getting him off it altogether, but that was again taken out of my hands. Michael had court appointed meetings with the city youth drug court on Wednesdays in our hometown that he and I both attended. I was on my way to pick him up, but passed him in his car.

"I turned around, and when we got to the meeting he told me that he had called and left a voicemail and that he would meet me there, but I did not receive it. He was doing great, he had some wonderfully supportive friends that he spent a lot of time with, and he seemed, to me, happier than he had been in years.

"He came over to our house the following Thursday and spent a couple of hours talking to Don and me about moving back home. I was ecstatic! His baby brother was five years old at the time, and as usual, Michael was carrying him around like he was his own child. They loved each other so much.

"When Michael got ready to leave, he kissed and hugged his little brother before putting him down. He walked to me and gave me a hug and kiss goodbye. I reminded him of the family camping trip we had planned for the weekend and asked him if he had thought anymore about coming with us. He told me he wanted to go, but would let me know for sure the following day. His little brother ran to him, jumped into his arms another time, and told Michael he required one more kiss goodbye. Michael, smiling the whole time, told his little brother, 'Don't worry buddy, I'll be back tomorrow.'

"The next day, Friday, I got a call from Michael's stepmother saying that he had run away. My mom drove over and picked up the two older boys. She and my dad were going to take them to our favorite campsite, and I would stay home and wait for the police to come and talk to me, and hopefully tell me they had found Michael who was safe and sound.

"I was out of my head and desperate to find him. I visited some of his friends, but no one had seen him. Sleep evaded me, while I hoped for a phone call from someone, anyone, saying he had returned home. Worry turned to anger. I wondered how Michael could do such a thing? Everything had been going so well, what would have caused him to run away?

"None of it made any sense to me and I grew angrier. I wanted to go camping with my family; the other boys were already there. Instead, I set out looking for him. I went to his friends' homes again, but none of them had seen him.

"Out of pure desperation, I went peering through windows of vacant homes up for sale, and every other imaginable place I thought he might be. I know it probably sounds crazy, even though Michael had gone missing and I felt an urgent need to find him, I knew in my heart that whatever caused him to leave and where ever he had gone, he would be back when he cooled off.

"I went back home to see if Michael had shown up there, but to my dismay, he had not. I could not sleep that night; I was so worried, and I was hoping for either a phone call (telling me) that he had returned to his dad's house, or that he would come to ours.

"I never heard from anyone and the police did not have any new information, so I set out looking for him again. I was exhausted and so confident that Michael would be home that I loaded my youngest son into the car and headed to the camp site without Don, asking him to call me on my cell when Michael showed up or when he heard anything."

Lee Ann drove the rest of the way to the campsite, exhausted both mentally and physically. As she recalls, she went straight to bed, but does not recollect ever falling asleep. The entire day was still a blur in her mind, but things were about to get much worse.

"From there, I'm going off my best recollection because it is all still a thick haze for me, even though it happened several years ago. I believe the time was about five o'clock Sunday morning. Someone was knocking on the door of my parent's camp trailer. I do not recall who opened the door, I think it was my mom, but I remember that Don was standing there.

"I immediately knew he had something bad to tell me because of the hour. He stepped into the trailer and said, 'They found Michael.'

"I started crying and asked if he was okay and all I heard was, 'No, he's dead.'

"I started screaming and punching Don. In that moment, I felt so much anger towards him, as irrational as that may sound. I eventually realized that I would have felt that way about anyone who had given such horrible news.

"I was angry about the way he told me. Later, I would find out that when the officers came to the house, they handed Don a piece of paper saying Michael had passed. He told me that over the course of several hours he had to pull off the road and read it several times to make sure he was giving me the right information.

"I think he was in shock. Don knew the general area that we were camping but there was so much territory to search, I don't know how he ever found us. He said he drove for five hours searching for us.

"I could hear weeping from my parents and turned to look at my youngest son and niece that were sleeping in the camper with us. Outside, I heard someone vomiting. The kids eventually woke up and while my family offered to tell them what had happened to their brother and cousin, I knew I had to be the one to tell them. It was the hardest thing I have ever had to do.

"We packed up and headed back home. I don't recall how we all got back, but I think my mom drove my car. It was on our way home I realized that my cell phone was not working and aside from getting ahold of Michael's dad to make sure this was a reality, I really did not care whether it was charged at all.

"I just wanted was for this to be some kind of nightmare I was going to wake up from, but by the time we got home people were already starting to show up at our house. That was when reality took hold, assuring me this was no nightmare."

At thirty-seven years of age, Lee Ann was faced with burying her oldest son. The pain and anguish she felt are beyond description. To say it was the most difficult thing in the world to do would be to misstate the unearthly emotional toll it took on her.

Mother Teresa was renowned for her compassion, but not many know that she sometimes struggled with her faith in God and Jesus. On more than one occasion, she admitted that she questioned God's presence in her life. Some would ask how such a woman of God could question His reality, but few people saw the despair, hunger, and fear she did daily.

As the days passed, Lee Ann began questioning her own faith. As pointed out in Charlett's story, it is unnatural for a parent to bury his or her child. Like Mother Teresa, the pain of losing her child was a physical and emotional strain, so much so, that the inevitable question of how a loving God could take a child from the world and leave behind unbearable pain.

After the funeral, all of Lee Ann's children, save the youngest, received grief counseling at school. She pointed out that she did not realize at the time that she was not providing direction for her kids, as she wallowed in her own grief. She would sit for hours staring at walls and thinking about everything that had occurred in her life may have contributed to Michael taking his own life.

"When Michael was in the rehab center in Utah, they explained to him that he should have a higher power in his 'recovery.' I recall one day, when I was down visiting him, he told me about it and asked, 'What if I don't believe in God?'

"To have him ask me this broke my heart, but my answer to him was that his higher power didn't necessarily have to be God. God, I explained, could be anything that he admired or loved such as nature, which he really loved and appreciated. How was I to know a short time later he would choose to drive his car up into the mountains to take his life? I still struggle with that fifteen and a half years later."

On top of the pain felt after losing her son, Lee Ann is faced with a tremendous amount of guilt. While trying to console and support him during recovery, she felt as though she might have contributed in some way to his seeking the place to end his life. All of us have engaged in conversations with loved ones who are no longer with us, but often our questions remain unanswered. Lee Ann's own soul searching still gnaws at her today, but she has somehow found acceptance in Michael's passing.

She slowly made her way through the overwhelming grief, and after two months decided she would return to work. It was then that she noticed her cell phone no longer worked; it was not that it wasn't merely charged as she initially thought. Before returning to the workforce, she thought it best to purchase a new phone.

"Two months after getting my new cell phone, I was walking into my office at work when I noticed there were some new voicemails, which was odd because I had not missed any calls. I was speaking with my parents as I put my code in to retrieve my voicemail and suddenly heard Michael's voice!

"The call he told me he placed months earlier, and subsequently left a voicemail I never received, came through on my new phone for the first time.

"I nearly fell to the floor when I heard his voice saying, 'Hi, mom.' I listened to it over and over. I let my parents listen to it, and then I listened to it some more. I couldn't concentrate at work that day thinking that it had to be a sign. I needed my faith back and this would be the beginning of my faith journey.

"I went straight home after work and immediately saved his message to a DVD through the microphone on our desktop computer. There was no way I would lose that precious voicemail again. Now I had his voice saved forever.

"A few mornings after the voicemail appeared on my phone, our youngest son walked downstairs and sat on my lap. He told he had a dream about Michael and that it was a good dream. He wanted to share it with me, and reassured me that it was good and that he did not want me to be sad.

"He proceeded to tell me that Michael had come to his room in the night and talked to him and told him he (Michael) had to go back to heaven. Lucas begged to go with him, and after some arguing Michael said he could take him for a little while, but he had to stay hidden because he wasn't a heaven boy. He told me heaven is so beautiful, and flowers grow right out of the clouds because there is no dirt. He said he saw two men he knew and that the girl angels were chasing Michael around.

"Tears streamed down my cheeks as my five-year-old was telling me about his dream. He sat on my lap wiping away my tears all while telling me about his dream. For him, everything was natural and as it should have been.

"As a result of the voicemail that strangely showed up in my phone months after Michael left it, and weeks after his death, followed by my five-year-old son's tale about visiting his older brother in Heaven, my faith began returning.

"Soon after Michael's death, the strange resurgence of his missing voicemail, and our baby's dream, our phone rang. Don reached to answer it and began to scream out. I knew immediately that we had lost another child. That kind of pain is only known and can be heard by those who have experienced it.

"Don's son had tragically passed away from a drug overdose. Irony can be more than strange, it can be cruel. Don's son that died was also named Michael. He was working making positive changes in his life, had checked into a rehabilitation center the last time I saw him, and was upbeat about getting his life on a straight path.

Unfortunately, he took a turn for the worst and his life spiraled out of control.

"When we went to Michael's funeral, we met his mother, Don's ex, there. She walked over to me and gave me a hug. I will never forget the words she said to me, 'I'm so sorry you have to go through this again.'

"All I could think of was that this beautiful lady was about to bury her son, and she was simultaneously grieving and concerned about me. I still cry when I think about that conversation, that moment in time. God, I believe, puts people in our lives for a reason, and she added tremendously to the faith that I was slowly reestablishing.

"I honestly don't know how Don and I survived, aside from having the other kids to take care of and love. We were both grieving different children and the same children all at the same time, but in different ways and at different stages. At best, grief is complicated when it is just one person, but our situation was nearly intolerable at times. I do know it made all of us appreciate and understand one another much more than we had in the past, and probably more than most people could ever possibly understand.

"That said, for us, because of the tragic ways our boys passed, it was very difficult to laugh, have fun, or even enjoy each other intimately without feeling guilty. Anything that our boys should have been experiencing seemed to destroy us as a couple; we were never in the same place emotionally, and I felt our relationship was going to suffer forever because I knew that we were forever changed. We were no longer the people we were before, and I knew grief lasted forever to some degree.

"Deep down, I also knew we would stay together because of what we had been through. Eventually, our senses of humor would return. Perhaps our humor was a little darker than before, but we could laugh and have fun.

Perhaps not as much fun as we used to, or as often as we once did, but we were making progress. I also knew I had to stop sugar coating everything for my kids in order to protect them.

"I tried and failed miserably when I lied to our youngest son about how his brother died. I did not believe he would know what suicide was at the age of five. The kids in his class told him the truth, and not only did he call me out on it, but it caused him to get ulcers."

Clearly I do not want to gloss over the death of Lee Ann's stepson. The grief, pain, and utter heartbreak felt, once again, by her family was mind numbing. As incredible as it may seem, her story does not end here. Once again, she and her husband will be forced to face reality on a scale many of us cannot comprehend.

"In 2007, Don got a great job offer. We had been struggling financially, and this was just what we needed to get us back on track. He went in for a work related physical, he hadn't had one for years, and his PSA blood test came back very high. Don was referred to a urologist that ordered more blood work and tests. He then had a biopsy that was reported as stage four prostate cancer.

"Once again, we were traumatized. After a consultation with the urologist, the only option was a radical prostatectomy that was to be scheduled immediately. The surgery would require several hours with numerous blood transfusions because it is such a blood-rich area of the body.

"My faith that was slowly returning began to waiver again, but when Don was in surgery, I prayed. I prayed more than I had ever prayed in my life, and for the first time in years I felt at peace. Surgery went well and after a very long recovery and dozens of radiation treatments, he was doing well enough to return to work.

"Life was still very difficult for us, especially around the holidays and birthdays, but we were finding our new normal. The kids were all doing well, and both of Don's boys were recently married. In fact, his oldest was married shortly after he finished his radiation treatments.

"Don's job would take him on the road from Utah to Arkansas, on to Texas, Oklahoma, all over the South. By 2010, all of our boys, with the exception of the youngest, were adults. A long-term job in Georgia would be his next assignment.

"My baby from my first marriage was nineteen, and I didn't want to leave him, but he didn't want to move from the only town he had ever known, and as difficult as it was, Don and I decided we needed to be together in Georgia.

"Our youngest didn't want to move either but he was twelve and had no choice in the matter. I developed a severe anxiety disorder after losing our two boys, and moving away from our other kids. Some days were excruciating, especially when I talked to them and I knew they were lonesome.

"My biggest fear had become losing another child. It happened twice and the thought of losing another was more than I could stand. If I wasn't thinking about Michael, I was worrying about the other boys. Though it seemed like we were doing well, there was always so much dread that crept into the recesses of my mind.

"I truly believed, and still believe that my faith is my guide. I prayed about every decision I had to make, and my life became so much easier and peaceful. In 2014, I started having horrible lower abdominal pains that I knew were gynecological in nature.

"My doctor was unable to find a reason for the excruciating pain, so in desperation, I changed doctors. After two years of no answers, my new doctor could not find a cause either. I did not want to take prescription pain medication, so as a result, he tried everything he could think of—from nerve damage medications to high dose ibuprofen.

"Nothing worked. In fact, the nerve pain medication made me act and feel drunk. I could not keep my balance nor could I walk straight, so I quit taking it. The next time my annual physical was due, I called to make an appointment, but my doctor had retired. I made an appointment with his much younger replacement, and he diagnosed me within five minutes. I would require a hysterectomy for fibroid tumors that had grown in size equivalent to that of a woman in her sixth month of pregnancy. I had the surgery in September.

"When I returned home, our youngest son had a series of seizures we later learned was brought on by stress. The trauma of losing his brother, stepbrother, seeing his mom and dad suffer through rounds of cancer and treatments had been enough to send him over the edge.

"In December of 2017, Don came home with a toothache and earache that had been bothering him for some time. He had seen our dentist and gotten a referral to see an oral surgeon to get some teeth pulled. He was at one doctor or another from then until April when he was referred to an ears, nose and throat specialist.

"The doctor noticed a little bump under his tongue and knew it needed to be biopsied, and once again we received bad news. The biopsy came back cancerous. He was diagnosed with head and neck cancer.

"We were referred to an amazing head & neck cancer surgeon in Atlanta. From the time, his doctors took biopsies up until it was time for his surgery. The tumor had grown from 3.5 cm to 7 cm. They knew in the first consultation that they would have to remove his tongue if the tumor crossed the midsections, and they were confident it had.

"We had hoped for a best-case scenario, since his symptoms had begun and the subsequent diagnosis was quickly made, but the opposite was our reality. The tumor had grown rapidly. He had a feeding tube placed before his throat surgery just in case he was not able to eat by mouth again. We were completely alone down here except for his cousin that lived North of Atlanta.

"After all of the testing and imaging, they decided to expedite his procedure, a twelve hour surgery, where they cut his throat from ear to ear to remove his tongue. The doctors cut a very large piece of tissue from his left thigh in order to construct a new tongue, or flap as they called it. His cousin came down and sat with me during the procedure; he was obviously worried about Don, but he also wanted to be sure that I was not alone while Don was being tended to by the medical team.

"I knew they would have to make a very large incision, but I was not prepared to see him cut from ear to ear. They had conducted a tracheotomy and, due to the trauma of the surgery, his eyes were black and nearly swollen shut. He had drain ports inserted in his neck and thigh. The sight of him in that state was horrifying.

"He was in intensive care for three days before being moved to the recovery area. They planned to release him July third, but on the second he started having abdominal pain and suffered from severe bleeding. For four excruciating days, the team of doctors worked on him to resolve the additional medical concerns. After the fourth day, I was able to take my husband home to allow him time to recover from this harrowing event."

Lee Ann detailed for me the difficulties in caring for her husband and young son who continued suffering from seizures. The sight of blood, the tracheotomy opening, and all the drain tubes made it hard on and for her, but she managed.

She told me that her strong faith in God got her through the worries and complications of caring for her husband. It also helped her deal with her son's unexpected medical concerns. You would think that after all had dealt with, Lee Ann's worries would end, but that was not to be. The world had one final bucket of pain to pour on her before it was finished.

"After Don's Family Medical Leave Act expired, his employment was terminated. When I say his employment was "terminated," I mean his employer sent him a message through a social media site telling him his services were no longer required. There we were, grieving, recovering from major medical procedures, and now we had no viable income.

"We took the COBRA supplemental insurance policy until we could get him on Medicare, but now my son and I are uninsured for the first time since I was nineteen years old. Don will probably never work again, and I have been looking for a job for over three months with no luck so far. At this writing, we have depleted our savings and are broke. Normally, I would be in a puddle on the floor, but as it stands, I feel that everything will be just fine. Our sons have decided to move in with us until we are back on our feet financially, and for that I am so very thankful.

"I still think about my Michael every single day. I miss our boys fiercely, but I know they are happy and not dealing with pain or grief. I am also content knowing I will get all the answers that I need one day. Perhaps not on this earth, but in Heaven, and I have come to terms with that. I also know we have helped a few people that were contemplating suicide and we have helped some people with addiction.

"I do not know what's in store for my future, but I do know that I wake up every morning with love, compassion, gratitude, my Heavenly Father and a crazy sense of humor in my heart and soul. These things get me through the day. All of this, and the blessings of our children and grandchildren, make life worthwhile.

National Suicide Hotline 1-800-273-8255
National Substance Abuse Hotline 1-800-662-HELP

Summary

In her book published in 1969, Elisabeth Kübler-Ross posited that humans pass through five stages while grieving or dealing with loss. She explained that, as a species, we move through these gates at different speeds, and in some cases, not in the precise order she outlined. Those stages, as she suggested, are 1. denial and isolation; 2. anger; 3. bargaining; 4. depression; 5. acceptance.

Denial and isolation are immediate reactions, Kübler-Ross offers, that help buffer us from the shock that we have lost a loved one. To deny their passing, or to isolate oneself is an attempt at avoiding the feeling of loneliness and feelings of helplessness. For some, there is a feeling of desperation; that the world has no value, and nothing is worth having or working to have.

Anger is the next phase of grieving. As the initial shock of losing someone begins to wear, lashing out at others, or possibly becoming angered at the deceased or loved one lost is natural. The feeling is natural, that is, as we struggle through the stages. Naturally, anger at the dead, or anyone not responsible for their passing, is irrational. Generally speaking, people understand this on some level, but oftentimes the logical portion of our mind is overcome by emotion.

Bargaining and guilt seem synonymous during this phase of grief. Many will bargain with God to bring their loved one back, although we know this is impossible. It is also at this stage we play the "what if" scenario. We sometimes ask ourselves, "What if I had prevented him/her from leaving," or "If only I had tried harder to make him or her feel worthy." This phase is a natural part of bargaining and, as stated previously, can manifest itself in the form of guilt.

A woeful sense of depression is often associated with the passing of a loved one. Depression can present itself in two forms: the practical and the more subtle. Facing mounting financial concerns can cause depression, or simply realizing our focus on this particular loss has caused us to lose sight of other things that need our focus and attention.

On a more subtle level is the depression associated with knowing our loved one is gone forever. This foreboding sense of grief can become overwhelming for some. Grief counselors can be instrumental in helping us move from this stage to the next.

Kübler-Ross tells us the final stage of grief is acceptance. Unfortunately, not everyone is allowed this portion of grief recovery, most especially if a loved one is taken from us suddenly and without warning. As humans, we tend to accept the inevitability of a loved one passing from a long-standing terminal illness, although we are still pained in our loss. When someone is taken from us suddenly, however, some will never come to accept their loss.

It is here that I would offer up a sixth stage: perseverance. I have always been a believer in the indomitable human spirit and the ability to overcome even the harshest and most wrenching of circumstances. Indeed, the surviving Jews of Nazi Germany overcame the worst mankind had to offer, as have countless peoples throughout human history.

We are an amazing species, capable of the cruelest acts, but also proficient in love, a Godly understanding of others, compassion, and a desire to keep pushing forward no matter the circumstances.

I am so happy that others have shared their stories with us, and have offered us each hope beyond the immediate misery they felt (and still feel). They have bared their souls and allowed us a glimpse inside their humanness. For that, we should all be thankful.

Note:

The author wishes to thank everyone who contributed to this work, most especially those who shared their stories and offered to us not just their pain, but also their desire to keep living and pushing forward.

Special thanks to Dr. Bridgette Hester for editing this work. You may not realize it, but you are amazing!

Lastly, thanks to you, Faithful Reader, for indulging me while I embarked into an arena of writing I never before considered. Without you, these are empty words on a still and silent page.

About the Author

Howard Upton is the critically acclaimed author of the Bill Evers action novels, *Of Blood and Stone* and *Occam's Razor*. He also penned a humorous compilation of talks he had with his little dog Rex, which he titled *My Dog's P.O.V. and How He Sees the World*.

In addition to these writing accomplishments, Howard has also contributed chapters to two other works, including *Go Ask Your Dad*, and *Secrets of the Martial Arts Masters, Volume 3*. Each of those books serve lofty purposes in helping others achieve some level of greatness within both dynamics, and he is proud of his small contributions to them.

When he is not writing, Howard is devoted to the traditional Japanese fighting arts of Yoshukai karate, judo, jujutsu, and kobudo (weapon arts), and teaches those same arts to a select group of students. His other hobbies include traveling and seeing the world (experiences he shares in his action novels), hiking, and backpacking, fishing, and spending his time with his gorgeous wife, Cathy.

Howard is a devoted husband, father, and grandfather whose life goals have all been met. You can purchase his books at his website www.howardupton.com as well as at all major on-line book retail outlets.

www.ingramcontent.com/pod-product-compliance
Lightning Source LLC
Chambersburg PA
CBHW070909280326
41934CB00008B/1643

* 9 7 8 1 9 4 6 8 1 1 0 5 9 *